第一课	Lesson One	你们好
第二课	Lesson Two	我叫王小明
第三课	Lesson Three	我的家
第四课	Lesson Four	我五岁
第五课	Lesson Five	我的好朋友
第六课	Lesson Six	我喜欢红色
第七课	Lesson Seven	我有红鞋子
第八课	Lesson Eight	我家有一只猫
第九课	Lesson Nine	我的眼睛在哪里
第十课	Lesson Ten	吃水果
节日(一)	Festival 1	圣诞节
节日(二)	Festival 2	中国新年

目录 Contents

第一课 你们好

Janet

王小明

李老师

Tom

你好!　你好!

老师好!　你们好!

一起来认字

你 you

你们 you (more than one person)

再见! 再见!

再见! 老师再见!

好 well, good	老师 teacher
你好 hello	再见 good-bye

第一课

一起来唱歌 🎵 51

(to the tune of *Twinkle Twinkle Little Star*)

你好，你好，你们好，
你好，你好，老师好。
Peter 好，Jane 好，Stephanie 好，
Jack 好，Mary 好，Graham 好，
你好，你好，你们好，
你好，你好，老师好。

一起来认字

Find, match and make a pair.
Use a different colour for each pair.
Tick the pairs you have found.

你好　hello ✓
老师　teacher
你们　you
再见　good-bye

你知道吗？ **Do you know?**

Do you know what these Chinese words are? 📢52

一　　二　　三

They are the Chinese numbers "one", "two" and "three".

Let's look at the Chinese numbers from one to ten below:

有多少？ How many?

第一课

一起来数数　How many? (1–10)

一起来听听 🔊 53

Count how many first. Then listen and circle the correct number.

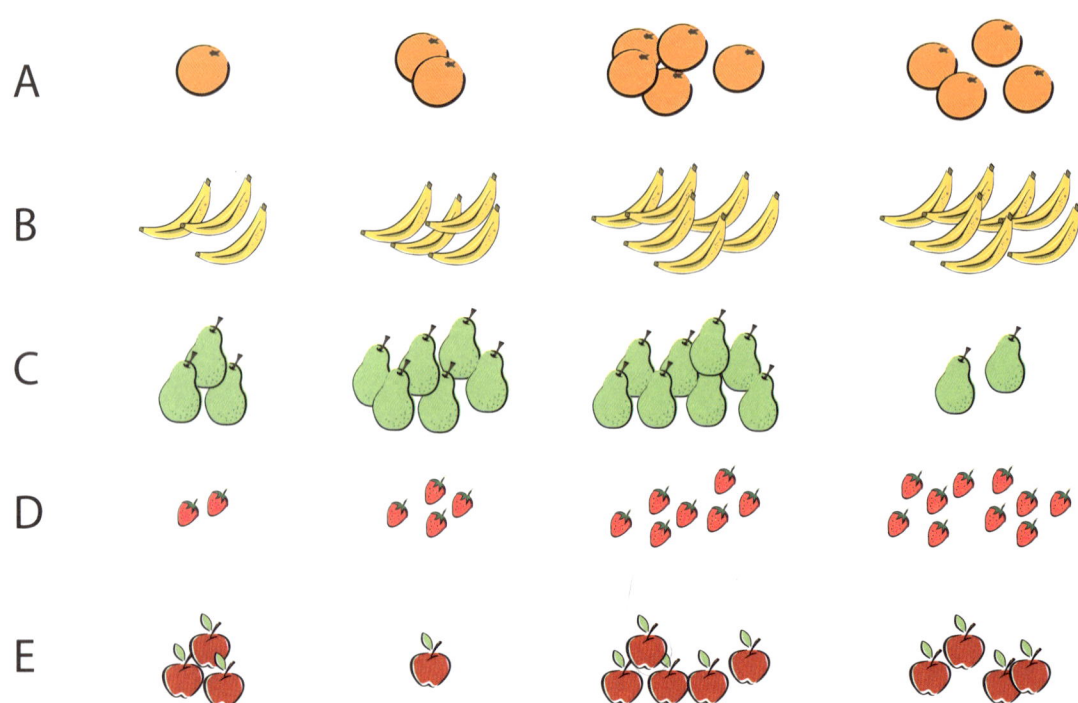

中文字笔画 Basic strokes

一起来写字　Practise writing these characters.

第二课 🔊54

我叫王

王小明

李苹

Janet

你好，
我叫王小明。

你好，
我叫李苹。

你好，王小明、李苹，我叫 ....。

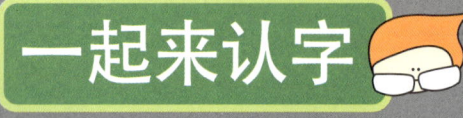 🔊55

我 I, me

叫 am/is/are called

小明

你叫什么？

我叫 _____ 。

我叫 _____ 。

李老师

Ridhi

Tom

Question words

我叫 I am called

你叫 you are called

什么 what

你叫什么？ What are you called?

8

第二课

一起来唱歌 🎵 56

(to the tune of *London Bridge*)

我叫王小明，王小明，王小明。
我叫王小明，我是小明。

我叫李苹，李苹，李苹。
我叫李苹，我是李苹。

一起来说话

Ask each other 你叫什么？and pick one of the pictures for your answer. After that ask each other again, giving your own name.

| Janet | Tom | 李苹 | Ridhi | 王小明 |

一起来听听 🔊 57

填上正确答案

Listen and write the correct question number in the box.

第二课

你知道吗？ Do you know?
Have you ever heard of the Giant Panda 大熊猫？
Have you seen one before?

白色 white

黑色 black

The giant panda is a well-loved animal in China. They eat bamboo shoots.

Colour in the picture on the right following the code below:

填色
你 – black
我 – white

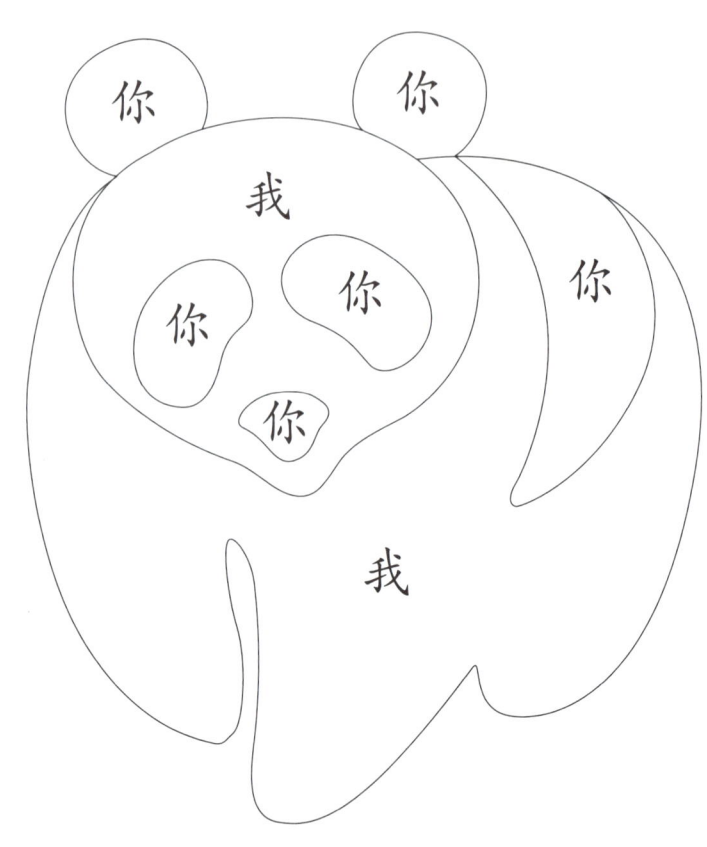

中文字笔画 Basic strokes

一起来写字

Now practise writing these characters.

第三课 🔊58

我的家

李苹的爸爸

李苹的妈妈

李苹的姐姐

我的家有四个人。

我有爸爸、妈妈和一个姐姐。

一起来认字

🔊59

我的 my	爸爸 dad
家 family	妈妈 mum
有 have	哥哥 older brother
	姐姐 older sister

13

我的家有五个人。

我有妈妈、哥哥、弟弟和妹妹。

王小明的妈妈

王小明的哥哥

王小明的弟弟

王小明的妹妹

弟弟 younger brother

妹妹 younger sister

和 and

Measure word

个　一个哥哥

　　三个姐姐

　　四个弟弟

　　五个妹妹

14

第三课

一起来听故事 🔊 60

爸爸买了梨回家。

妈妈叫孩子们分梨吃。

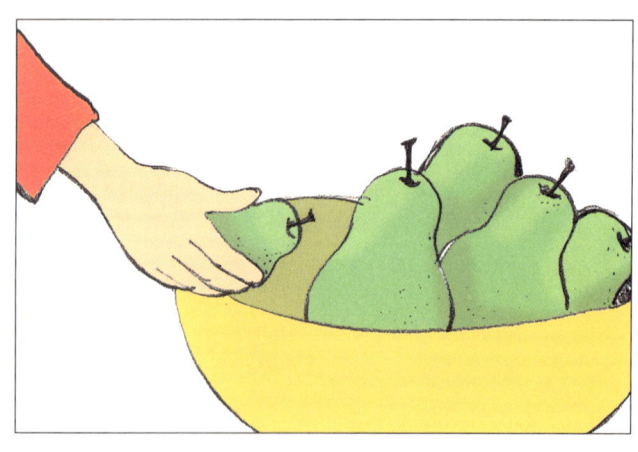

孔融拿了最小的梨。

孔融的哥哥姐姐拿梨吃。

孔融的弟弟妹妹拿梨吃。

爸爸妈妈说孔融是好孩子。

一起来说话

王小明的家有几个人？	How many people are there in Siu Ming's family?
王小明的家有谁？	Who are they?
李苹的家有几个人？	How many people are there in Lei Ping's family?
李苹的家有谁？	Who are they?

用线连起来

Use a red pen to link 王小明 with his family.
Use a green pen to link 李苹 with her family.

王小明的妈妈

李苹的爸爸

王小明的弟弟

李苹

王小明

李苹的姐姐

王小明的哥哥

李苹的妈妈

王小明的妹妹

第三课

画图 Draw your family inside the house.

一起来说话

介绍你的家人

Now introduce your family to your class.

中文字笔画 Basic strokes

一起来写字

Now practise writing these characters.

第四课 🔊 62

我五岁

王小明

李苹

Janet

Tom

王小明：李苹，你几岁？
李苹：　我五岁，你几岁？
王小明：我六岁。

Tom：　Janet，你几岁？
Janet：我七岁，你几岁？
Tom：　我八岁。

一起来认字

🔊 63

沒有 do not have

岁 year (age)　　他 he

几岁 how old　　她 she

Question words

几 How many

吗

我有一个姐姐,她九岁。

我没有姐姐。
我有一个哥哥,他十岁;
我有一个弟弟,他三岁。

你几岁?	我六岁。
How old are you?	I am six years old.
你有几个哥哥?	一个。
How many older brothers have you got?	One.
你有妹妹吗?	有。
Do you have a younger sister?	Yes I have.

第四课

一起来说话 🔊 64

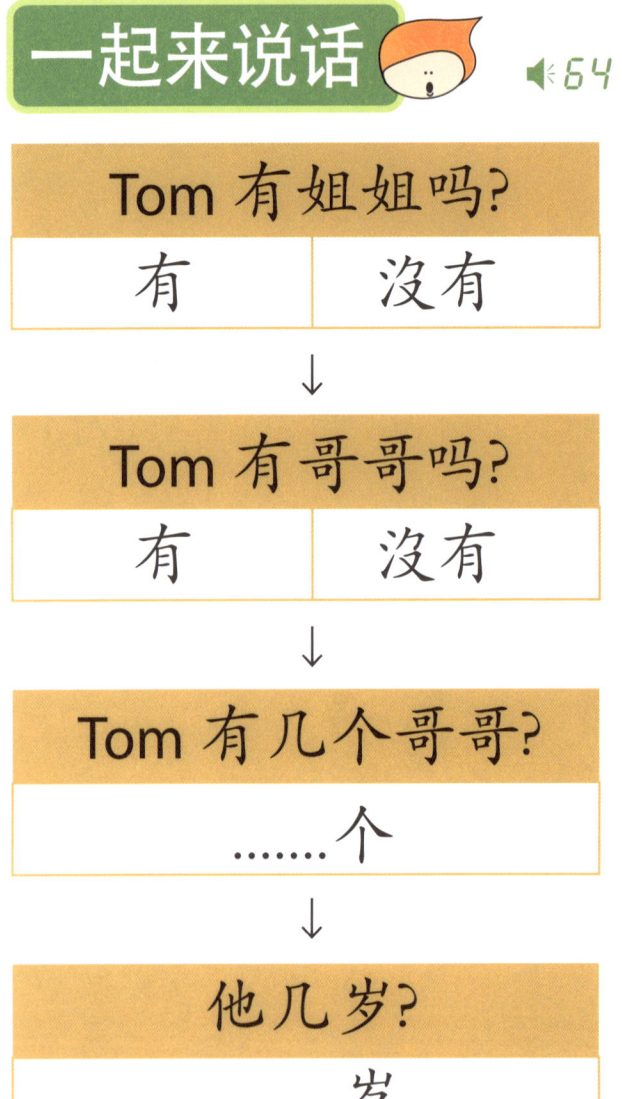

圈出正确答案

Now about your family: circle your answers.

你有哥哥吗?	有	沒有	他几岁?	............岁
你有姐姐吗?	有	沒有	她几岁?	............岁
你有弟弟吗?	有	沒有	他几岁?	............岁
你有妹妹吗?	有	沒有	她几岁?	............岁

用线连起来

Look at the pictures on page 19 and page 20.
Draw a line to join the person to his/her age.

李苹　　　王小明　　　Tom　　　Janet　　　李苹的姐姐

| 九岁 | 六岁 | 五岁 | 七岁 | 八岁 |

一起来听听 🔊 65

用线连起来

Listen and draw a line to link the correct age with the right person.

Janet's 的爸爸　　　Janet's 的妈妈

Janet's 的哥哥　　　Janet　　　Janet's 的姐姐

Janet's 的弟弟　　　Janet's 的妹妹

九岁　　一岁　　七岁　　十岁　　四岁

第四课

找找看

姐姐

再见

我五岁

我	四	老	师	大
五	家	爸	爸	五
岁	你	好	弟	弟
二	姐	姐	小	李
八	哥	我	再	见
岁	哥	几	六	十
妈	的	有	叫	岁
妈	什	妹	妹	么

弟弟

哥哥

爸爸

老师

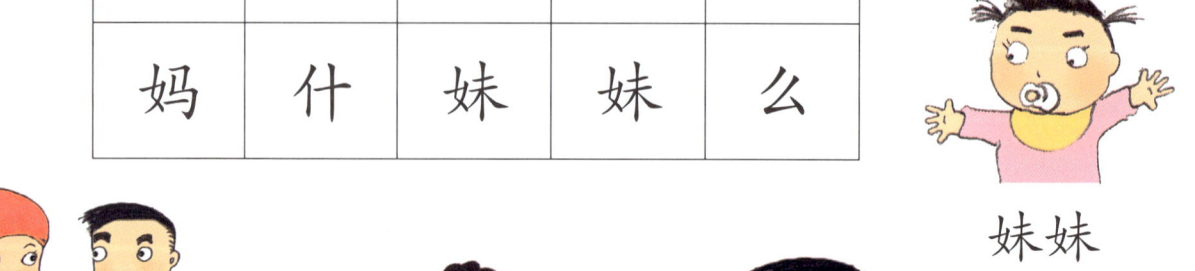
妹妹

你好

妈妈

我六岁

中文字笔画 Basic strokes

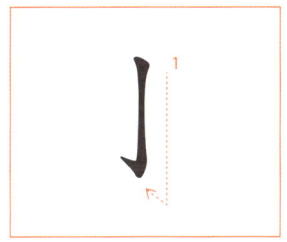    

一起来写字

Now practise writing these characters.

Which one is big and which one is small?

24

第五课 🔊66 我的好

王小明

王小师

李苹

这是我的朋友，她叫Janet。

这是我的哥哥，他叫王小师。

一起来认字

🔊67

这 this

是 is

这是 this is

我的 my

朋友 friend

我们 we

好朋友 good friend

朋友

我们是好朋友。

Janet

Ridhi

Tom

Question words

谁 who	这是谁？ Who is this?
	这是我的弟弟。 This is my younger brother.
谁的 whose	这是谁的姐姐？ Whose older sister is this?
	这是李苹的姐姐。 This is Li Ping's older sister.

26

第五课

一起来说话  这是谁?

 Janet's family

 王小明有三个朋友

Janet　　　　　　　Ridhi　　　　　　　Tom

这是谁?	她/他叫什么?
这是王小明的好朋友_____。	她/他叫_____。

一起来唱歌 🔊 68

(to the tune of *London Bridge*)

> 这是我的好朋友，好朋友，好朋友，
> 这是我的好朋友，她叫李苹。

 Janet
 Tom
 李苹
 Ridhi
 王小明

一起来说话  画图

Draw a picture of a friend and show it to your class.
Introduce your friend as: 这是我的朋友，他/她叫................，他/她............岁。

第五课

一起来听故事 🔊69

小小和大大是好朋友。

一天,小小和大大在树林里玩。

忽然,一只黑熊走出来,小小和大大连忙逃跑。

大大跑得快,他爬到树上去。

小小跑得慢,快要被黑熊追上了。

小小倒在地上装死,黑熊上前闻闻小小,以为他死了就走开了。

大大从树上下来,问小小大熊在他耳边说什么。

小小告诉大大,黑熊说:"有危险时不顾朋友,自己跑掉,这就不是好朋友。"

中文字画笔 Basic strokes

This is a basic box shape. It can be square or rectangular:

Most boxes have things inside them:

一起来写字

Now practise writing these characters.

第六课 我喜欢

🔊 70

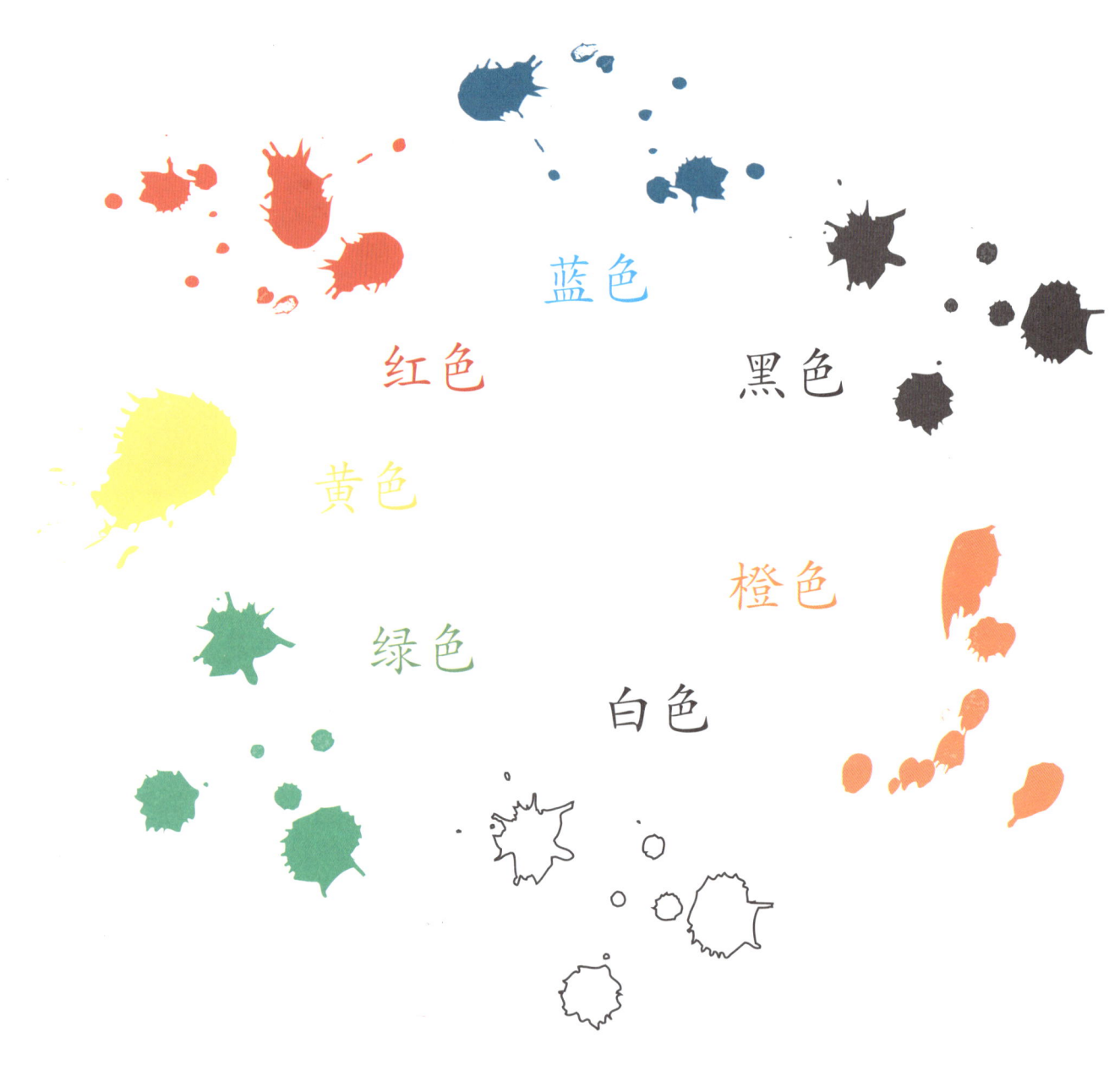

蓝色
红色
黑色
黄色
橙色
绿色
白色

一起来认字

🔊 71

颜色 colour
红色 red
橙色 orange
黄色 yellow
绿色 green

红色

我喜欢绿色。
你喜欢什么颜色?

我喜欢红色。

我喜欢橙色和白色。
你喜欢什么颜色?

我喜欢黄色和蓝色。

蓝色 blue　　　白色 white

黑色 black　　　喜欢 like

第六课

一起来认字

配对 Match the colours with the correct characters.

橙色 ☐   黑色 ☐   绿色 ☐   白色 ☐
蓝色 ☐   红色 ☐   黄色 ☐

填色
Colour in the characters.

黑　红　蓝　　黄　白　颜色
橙　　　绿

一起来唱歌 🎵 72

(to the tune of *This Old Man*)

香蕉，真好吃，
黄色香蕉真好吃，
哥哥喜欢吃香蕉，
一连吃了十多个。

苹果，真好吃，
红色苹果真好吃，
妹妹喜欢吃苹果，
一连吃了十多个。

绿色梨子 / 爸爸 / 十多个

画图 Colour in the picture

Draw a fruit of this colour 黄色
用黄色画一个水果

Draw a cat of this colour 黑色
用黑色画一只猫

Draw a flower of this colour 橙色
用橙色画一朵花

Draw a leaf of this colour 绿色
用绿色画一片叶子

第六课

一起来听听  🔊 73

勾出每个人喜欢的颜色
Tick the colours for each person.

一起来说话

李老师喜欢什么颜色？

你喜欢什么颜色？ Which colour do you like?
问你班上的同学。 Ask your friends in the class.

一起来写字

Do you remember these basic strokes?

| 一 | 丨 | 丿 | 乀 | 丶 | 丿 |

Now practise writing these characters.

土 一 十 土 土 土 土 土 土 土

火 丶 丿 灬 火 火 火 火 火 火

数一数 Let's count

把适当数字写在空格里。Write the correct numbers in the boxes.
有几个人？ How many people?

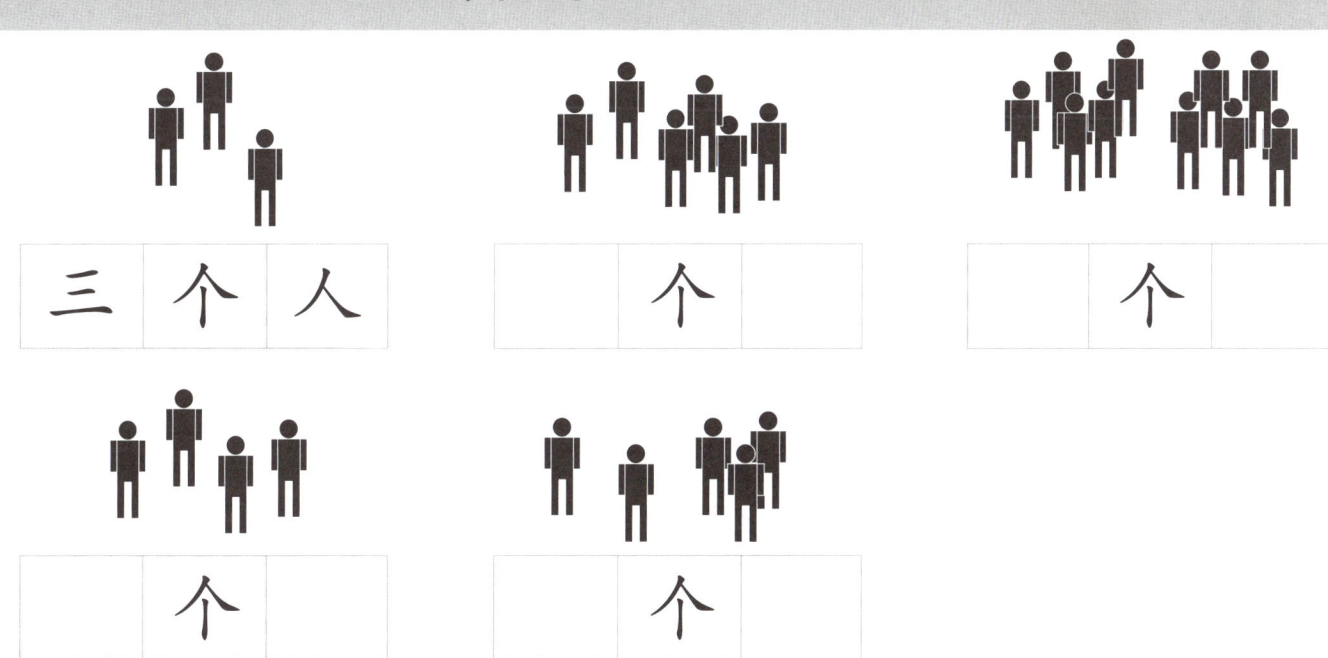

| 三 | 个 | 人 |

| | 个 | |

| | 个 | |

| | 个 | |

| | 个 | |

第七课 🔊74

我有红

我有：  汗衫

 毛衣

 裤子

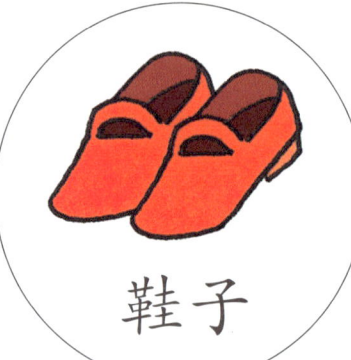 鞋子

我有裙子。

一起来认字

🔊75

鞋子 shoes　　　裤子 trousers

汗衫 T-shirt　　　毛衣 jumper

　　　　　　　　裙子 dress/skirt

鞋子

我有一双红鞋子。 我有一件绿毛衣。

红鞋子 red shoes		绿毛衣 green jumper	
蓝裙子 blue skirt		黑裤子 black trousers	

Measure words

一条　　一条裤子

一件　　一件毛衣 / 一件汗衫

一双　　一双鞋子

第七课

一起来说话 颜色 + 衣服 = ? Colour + clothes =

例:  +  =  蓝裤子

 + =

 + =

 + =

告诉我 Tell me

爸爸有  ……………………………。

妈妈有  ……………………………。

姐姐有  ……………………………。

王小明有  ……………………………。

我有  ……………………………。

一起来听故事 🔊76

李苹有一件黄汗衫。

李苹的姐姐有一条蓝裙子。

李苹的爸爸有一条白裤子。

妈妈洗衣服。

洗衣机停了。

看看他們的衣服!
李苹的黄汗衫。

姐姐的蓝裙子。

爸爸的……………。

第七课

一起来说话  他们穿什么?
What are they wearing?

王小明的哥哥　　王小明的妹妹　　王小明的妈妈　　王小明的弟弟　　王小明

这是谁的毛衣?
Whose jumper is this?

王小明 ☐　　妈妈 ☐
哥哥 ☐　　弟弟 ☐　　妹妹 ☐

这是谁的裤子?
Whose trousers are these?

王小明 ☐　　妈妈 ☐
哥哥 ☐　　弟弟 ☐　　妹妹 ☐

这是谁的汗衫?
Whose T-shirt is this?

王小明 ☐　　妈妈 ☐
哥哥 ☐　　弟弟 ☐　　妹妹 ☐

这是谁的裙子?
Whose skirt is this?

王小明 ☐　　妈妈 ☐
哥哥 ☐　　弟弟 ☐　　妹妹 ☐

中文字笔画 Basic strokes

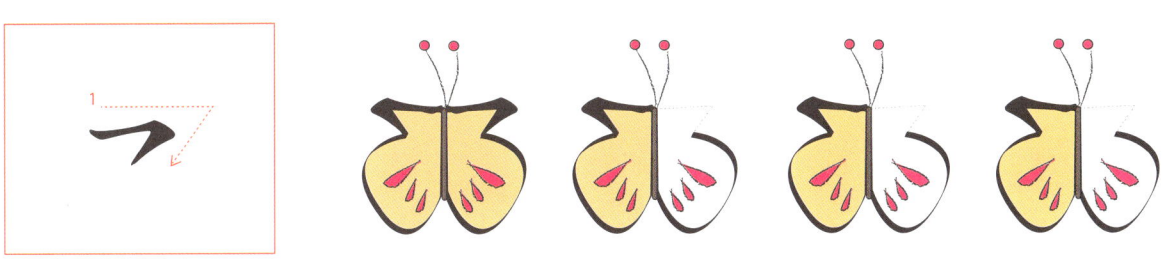

Do you remember these basic strokes?

| 丶 | 一 | 丿 | 乚 | 丶 | 亅 |

Now practise writing these characters.

衣	丶	二	亠	亍	衣	衣	衣	衣	衣
衣	衣	衣	衣	衣	衣	衣	衣	衣	衣
子	乛	了	子	子	子	子	子	子	子

Now find 亻、口、女、土、子 in the following characters and circle these elements.

42

第八课 🔊77

我家有

我家有一只猫，
它叫Lily。

我家有一只狗，
它叫Dong Dong。

我家有一只鸟，
它叫Ding Ding。

一起来认字 🔊78

狗 dog	鸟 bird
牛 cow	鱼 fish
猫 cat	羊 sheep	它 it

一只猫

我有一只黑猫。

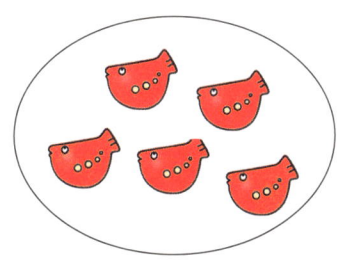

我有三只蓝鸟。

我有五条红鱼。

黑猫 	白羊 	红鱼 
黄狗 	黄牛 	蓝鸟 

Measure words

一只　　一只猫 / 一只狗 / 一只鸟

一条　　一条鱼

一头　　一头牛

第八课

一起来唱歌

(to the tune of *Old MacDonald had a farm*)

李苹妹妹有只猫

（一）李苹妹妹有只猫，依呀依呀呦。
它在树上轻轻叫，依呀依呀呦。
猫在这里叫，猫在那里叫，
喵喵喵，喵喵喵，到处都是喵喵，
李苹妹妹有只猫，依呀依呀呦。

（二）王小明有一只狗，依呀依呀呦。
它在树下蹦蹦跳，依呀依呀呦。
狗在这里叫，狗在那里叫，
汪汪汪，汪汪汪，到处都是汪汪，
王小明有一只狗，依呀依呀呦。

（三）牛

（四）羊

一起来说话

数一数，有多少？ Count how many, say it first then write the correct number in the boxes.

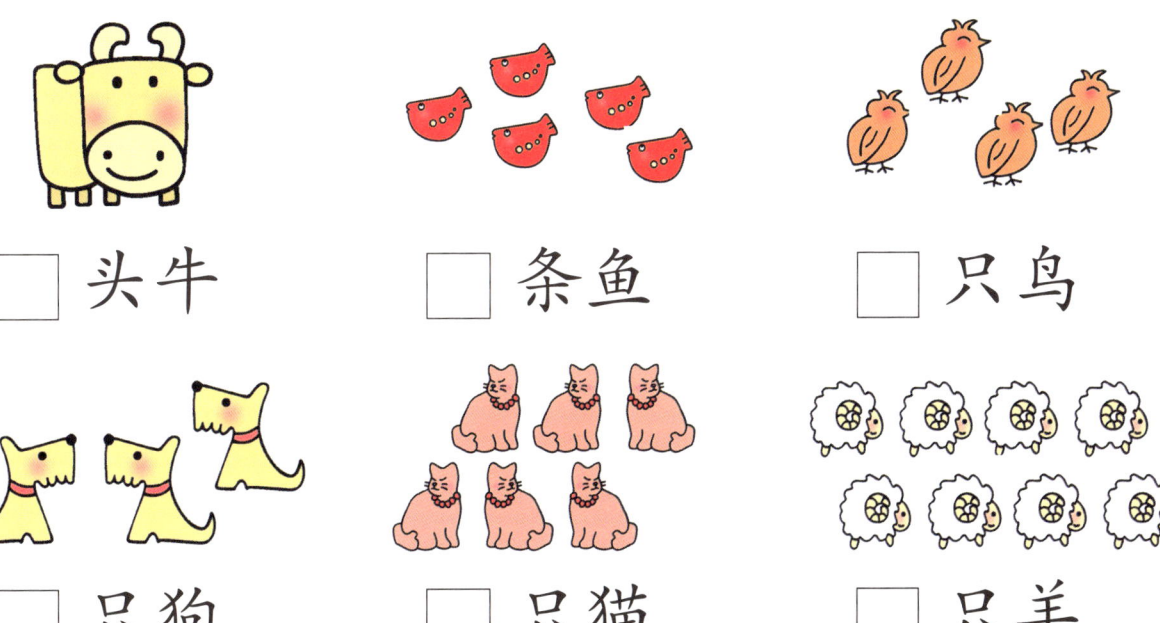

□ 头牛　　□ 条鱼　　□ 只鸟

□ 只狗　　□ 只猫　　□ 只羊

王小明家有什么？

王小明家有一只猫和一只狗。

李苹家有什么？

你家有什么？

第八课

一起来听听 🔊 80

画线连起来 Draw a line to link the animal to its owner.

在括号内加 √ 或 ×。
Now listen to the recording and put in either √ or ×. 🔊 81

一起来写字

Do you remember these basic strokes?

ノ	一	丨	丶	ノ

Now practise writing these characters.

一起来数数

在空格内填上正确中文字

Now try filling in the blanks.

| | 件 | 毛 | |

| | 只 | 狗 |

| | 头 | |

| | 个 |

第九课 🔊 82

我的眼

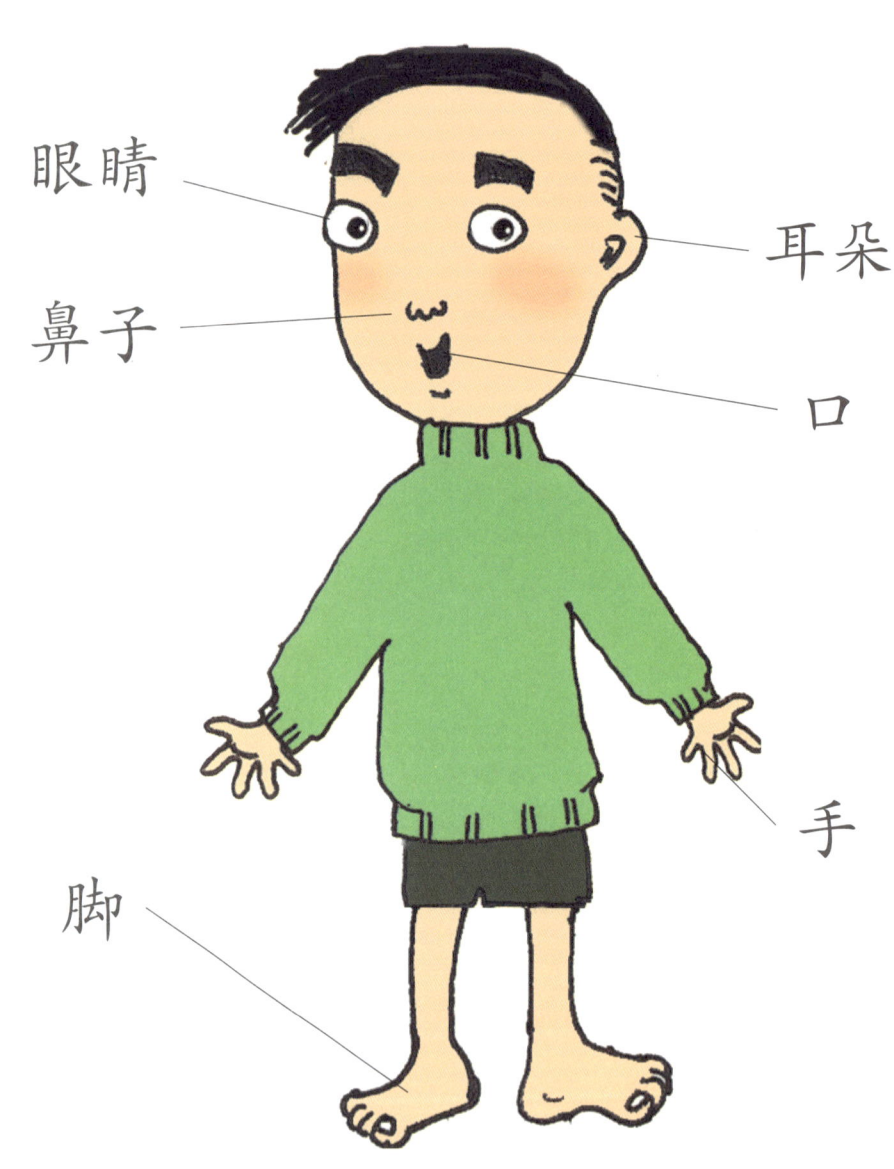

一起来认字

🔊 83

鼻子 nose　　脚 feet

眼睛 eye　　口 mouth　　这里 here

耳朵 ear　　手 hand　　在 is

睛在哪里

我的眼睛在哪里？
我的眼睛在这里。   我的耳朵在哪里？

我的手在哪里？

Measure words

一个   一个口 / 一个鼻子

一双   一双眼睛 / 一双耳朵 / 一双手 / 一双脚

Question words

哪里 where

你的眼睛在哪里？ Where are your eyes?

50

第九课

一起来认字

填上适当颜色：

Colour in the features as directed.

我有蓝色眼睛

我有绿色鼻子

我有橙色口

我有红色耳朵

把适当的英文字母填在空格内

Write the correct letter in the boxes.

口	A
手	B
眼睛	C
耳朵	D
脚	E
鼻子	F

一起来说话

画出不见了的部分 Draw the missing parts.

第九课

一起来听故事 谁最有用?

小明的眼睛、耳朵、鼻子、口、手和脚吵起架来,他们都说自己最有用。

一天,小明在花园里玩耍。忽然闻到一些焦味,便立刻循著焦味走去看看。

他看见邻居的车房着火了,还有人叫救命。

小明连忙跑回家中,大声叫妈妈,告诉她邻居车房着火了。

妈妈立刻报警,邻居跑到车房,把孩子救出来。

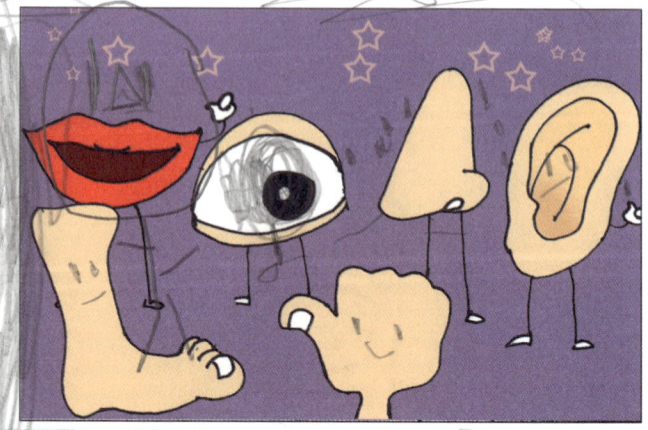

小明的眼睛、耳朵、鼻子、口、手和脚不吵架了。你说他们当中谁最有用?

基本字形 Basic shapes

Like a tunnel, this shape is a rectangle with an open bottom.
The tunnel can be wide or it can be narrow:

These tunnels have things inside them:

同 月

| 月 | 丿 | 冂 | 月 | 月 | 月 | 月 | 月 | 月 | 月 |

Now practise writing this character.

Can you find 口, 日 and 月 in the following characters?
Circle all the 口 with a blue pen, all the 日 with a red pen
and all the 月 with a green pen.

叫　明　哥　有　和　是　裙

第十课 🔊85

吃水果

 草莓

 香蕉

水果

 苹果

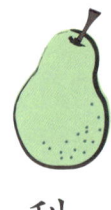 梨　　 西瓜　　 橙子

我喜欢吃水果！

一起来认字　🔊86

苹果 apple	草莓 strawberry
吃 eat	西瓜 watermelon	香蕉 banana
水果 fruit	梨 pear	橙子 orange

55

你喜欢吃什么水果?

 王小明

我喜欢吃苹果。

 Janet

我喜欢吃西瓜。

 Ridhi

我喜欢吃梨。

 Tom

我喜欢吃草莓。

我喜欢吃橙子。  李老师

Measure words

一只　一只香蕉

一个　一个橙子 / 一个西瓜 / 一个苹果 / 一个梨

Question words

什么 what

什么水果? What fruit?　吃什么水果? To eat what fruit?

你喜欢吃什么水果? What fruit do you like to eat?

第十课

一起来唱歌 🎵 87

(to the tune of Twinkle twinkle little star)

我是一个大苹果，又香又甜又好吃。
大人小孩都爱我，说我是个好宝宝。
一天吃一个苹果，身体健康十分好。

一起来说话

你喜欢吃什么水果？

我喜欢吃 —— 香蕉
　　　　　　 草莓
　　　　　　 梨和橙子
　　　　　　 西瓜和苹果

王小明喜欢吃什么水果？

王小明
爸爸
妈妈　　喜欢吃
哥哥
姐姐

Which fruit do your friends like to eat?

一起来数数

☐ 个苹果

☐ 个香蕉

☐ 个西瓜

☐ 个橙子

一起来听听

🔊 88 谁喜欢吃什么水果？

a 　　b 　　c

d 　　e 　　f

王小明 .... Ridhi ....

Tom .... Janet ....

李苹 .... 李老师 ....

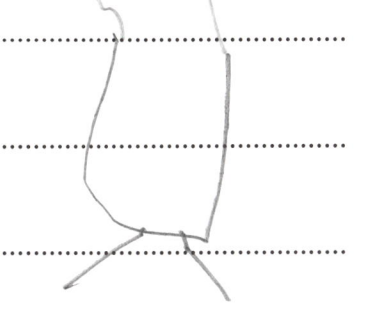

第十课

什么颜色？

用线把颜色和水果连起来
Draw a line to link the colour to the fruit.

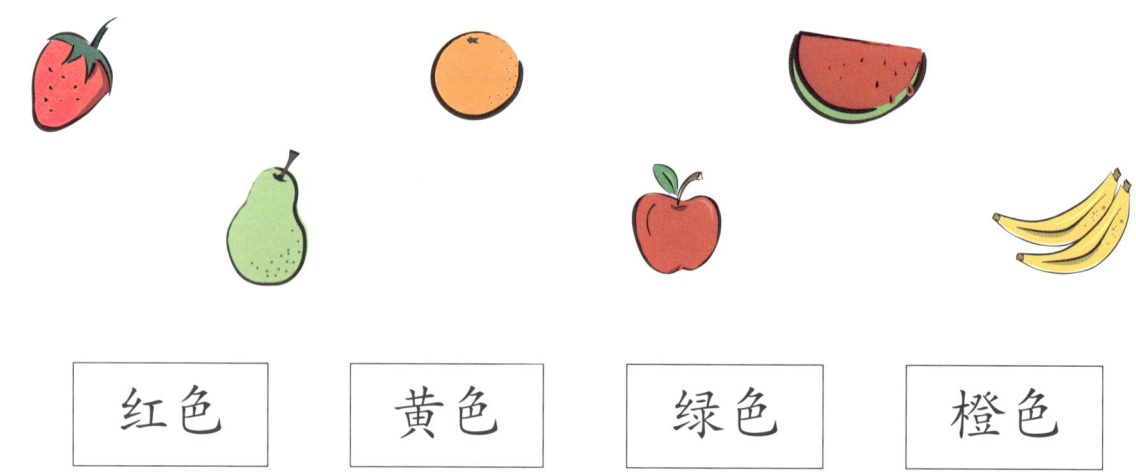

| 红色 | 黄色 | 绿色 | 橙色 |

填色 Colour the shapes.

中文字笔画 Basic strokes

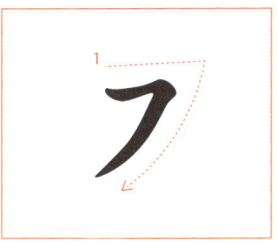    

一起来写字

Do you remember these basic strokes?

| 亅 | 丿 | 乀 | 一 | 丨 | 乛 | 乙 |

Now practise writing these characters.

Now try filling in the blanks.

| | | 果 |  | | 我 | 的 | 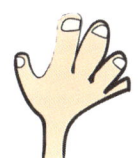 |

节日（一） 🔊 89　　　　　　圣诞节

圣诞快乐！

大家唱圣诞歌。

一起来认字 🔊 90

圣诞节　Christmas

圣诞老人　Father Christmas

圣诞树　Christmas tree

圣诞老人送礼物!

圣诞树

大家 everyone	
快乐 happy	送 to give out
礼物 present	唱歌 to sing

节日（一）

王小明家的圣诞树

把适当的字母写在横线上

Whose present is it? Write the correct letter next to the person.

找找看

Can you find these from the table above?

1. Father Christmas
   圣诞老人

2. Christmas tree
   圣诞树

3. Dad's present
   爸爸的礼物

4. Merry Christmas
   圣诞快乐

5. Christmas
   圣诞节

6. sing
   唱歌

圣	诞	老	人	我
叫	诞	的	家	们
圣	一	快	字	吃
诞	唱	好	乐	圣
节	歌	个	再	诞
字	弟	爸	见	树
爸	爸	的	礼	物

节日（二） 🔊91　　　　　　中国新

一起来认字 🔊92

新年	New Year
糖果	sweets
红包	red packet

年

我喜欢吃糖果和年糕。

中国新年 Chinese New Year

年糕 New Year rice cake

中国 China/Chinese

节日（二）

一起来听故事 年兽的故事 🔊93

可怕的年兽

年兽害人

年兽怕光

年兽怕声

年兽怕红色

年兽不再来了

一起来唱歌 🎵 94

(to the tune of *Happy Birthday*)

祝你新年快乐，祝你新年快乐，
恭喜大家发财，祝你新年快乐！

一起来说话

李苹喜欢吃什么？　　王小明喜欢吃什么？
Tom 喜欢吃什么？　　Ridhi 喜欢吃什么？

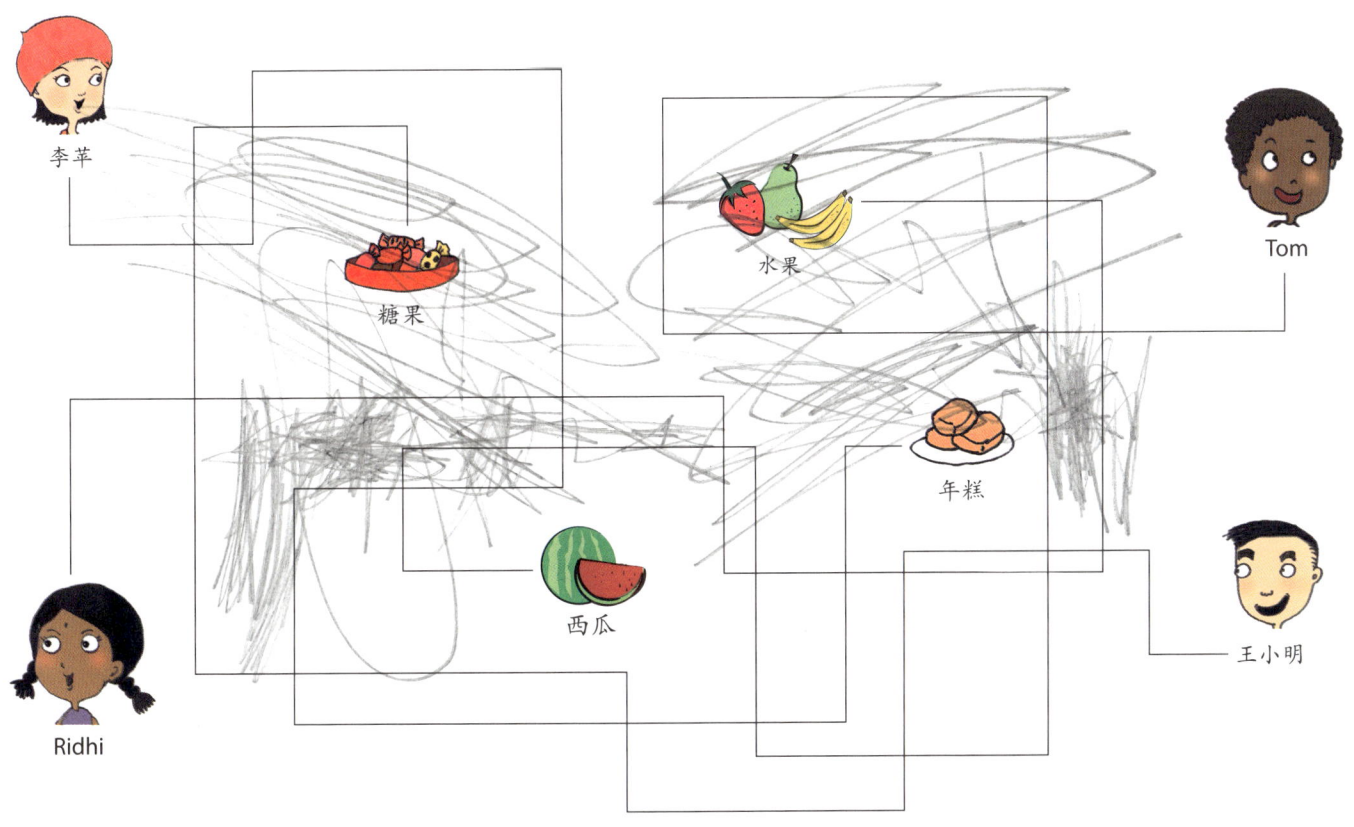

Vocabulary

Vocabulary	English meaning	Putonghua pinyin	Cantonese jyutping
CHAPTER 1			
你	you	nǐ	nei[5]
你们	you (more than one person)	nǐ men	nei[5] mun[4]
好	well, good	hǎo	hou[2]
你好	hello	nǐ hǎo	nei[5] hou[2]
老师	teacher	lǎo shī	lou[5] si[1]
再见	good-bye	zài jiàn	zoi[3] gin[3]
一	one	yī	jat[1]
二	two	èr	ji[6]
三	three	sān	saam[1]
四	four	sì	sei[3]
五	five	wǔ	ng[5]
六	six	liù	luk[6]
七	seven	qī	cat[1]
八	eight	bā	baat[8]
九	nine	jiǔ	gau[2]
十	ten	shí	sap[6]
CHAPTER 2			
我	I, me	wǒ	ngo[6]
叫	am/is/are called	jiào	giu[3]
我叫	I am called	wǒ jiào	ngo[5] giu[3]
你叫	you are called	nǐ jiào	nei[5] giu[3]
什么	what	shén me	saam[6] mo[1]
你叫什么	what are you called	nǐ jiào shén me	nei[5] giu[3] saam[6] mo[1]
白色	white	bái sè	baak[6] sik[1]
黑色	black	hēi sè	haak[1] sik[1]
CHAPTER 3			
我的	my	wǒ de	ngo[5] dik[1]

Vocabulary	English meaning	Putonghua pinyin	Cantonese jyutping
家	family	jiā	gaa[1]
有	have	yǒu	jau[5]
爸爸	dad	bà ba	baa[1] baa[1]
妈妈	mum	mā ma	maa[1] maa[1]
哥哥	older brother	gē ge	go[1] go[1]
姐姐	older sister	jiě jie	ze[2] ze[2]
弟弟	younger brother	dì di	dai[6] dai[6]
妹妹	younger sister	mèi mei	mui[6] mui[6]
和	and	hé	wo[4]
个	a measure word	gè	go[3]

CHAPTER 4

岁	year (age)	suì	seoi[3]
几岁	how old	jǐ suì	gei[2] seoi[3]
没有	do not have	méi yǒu	mut[6] jau[5]
他	he	tā	taa[1]
她	she	tā	taa[1]
几	how many	jǐ	gei[2]
吗	a question word	ma	maa[1]

CHAPTER 5

这	this	zhè	ze[2]
是	is	shì	si[6]
这是	this is	zhè shì	ze[2] si[6]
我的	my	wǒ de	ngo[5] dik[1]
朋友	friend	péng yǒu	pang[4] jau[5]
我们	we	wǒ men	ngo[5] mun[4]
好朋友	good friend	hǎo péng yǒu	hou[2] pang4 jau[5]
谁	who	shéi	seoi[4]
谁的	whose	shéi de	dik[1]

Vocabulary

Vocabulary	English meaning	Putonghua pinyin	Cantonese jyutping
CHAPTER 6			
颜色	colour	yán sè	ngaan[4] sik[1]
红色	red	hóng sè	hung[4] sik[1]
橙色	orange	chéng sè	caang[2] sik[1]
黄色	yellow	huáng sè	wong[4] sik[1]
绿色	green	lǜ sè	luk[6] sik[1]
蓝色	blue	lán sè	laam[4] sik[1]
黑色	black	hēi sè	haak[1] sik[1]
白色	white	bái sè	baak[6] sik[1]
喜欢	like	xǐ huān	hei[2] fun[1]
CHAPTER 7			
鞋子	shoes	xié zi	haai[4] zi[2]
汗衫	T-shirt	hàn shān	hon[6] saam[1]
裤子	trousers	kù zi	fu[3] zi[2]
毛衣	jumper	máo yī	mou[4] ji[1]
裙子	skirt	qún zi	kwan[4] zi[2]
CHAPTER 8			
猫	cat	māo	maau[1]
狗	dog	gǒu	gau[2]
牛	cow	niú	ngau[4]
羊	sheep	yang	joeng[4]
鸟	bird	niǎo	niu[5]
鱼	fish	yú	jyu[4]
它	it	tā	taa[1]

Vocabulary	English meaning	Putonghua pinyin	Cantonese jyutping
CHAPTER 9			
眼睛	eye	yǎn jing	ngaan^5 zing^1
耳朵	ear	ěr duo	ji^5 do^2
鼻子	nose	bí zi	bei^6 zi^2
口	mouth	kǒu	hau^2
手	hand	shǒu	sau^2
脚	feet	jiǎo	goek^3
这里	here	zhè li	ze^2 leoi^5
在	is	zài	zoi^6
哪里	where	nǎ li	naa3 leoi^5
CHAPTER 10			
吃	eat	chī	hek^3
水果	fruit	shuǐ guǒ	seoi^2 gwo^2
苹果	apple	píng guǒ	ping^4 gwo^2
西瓜	water melon	xī guā	sai^1 gwaa^1
梨	pear	lí	lei^2
草莓	strawberry	cǎo méi	cou^2 mui^2
香蕉	banana	xiāng jiāo	hoeng^1 ziu^1
橙子	orange	chéng zi	caang^2 zi^2
CHRISTMAS			
圣诞节	Christmas	shèng dàn jié	sing^3 daan^3 zit^3
圣诞老人	Father Christmas	shèng dàn lǎo rén	sing^3 daan^3 lou^5 jan^4
圣诞树	Christmas tree	shèng dàn shù	sing^3 daan^3 syu^6
快乐	happy	kuài le	faai^3 lok^6
礼物	present	lǐ wù	lai^5 mat^6
大家	everybody	dà jiā	daai^6 gaa^1
送	to give out	sòng	sung^3
唱歌	to sing	chàng gē	coeng^3 go^1

Vocabulary

Vocabulary	English meaning	Putonghua pinyin	Cantonese jyutping
CHINESE NEW YEAR			
中国	China/Chinese	zhōng guó	zung[1] gwok[3]
新年	new year	xīn nián	san[1] nin[4]
糖果	sweets	táng guǒ	tong[4] gwo[2]
红包	red packet	hóng bāo	hung[4] baau[1]
年糕	New Year rice cake	nián gāo	nin[4] gou[1]
MEASURE WORDS			
一个		yī gè	jat[1] go[3]
一个妹妹	a younger sister	yī gè mèi mei	jat[1] go[3] mui[6] mui[6]
一个口	a mouth	yí gè kǒu	jat[1] go[3] hau[2]
一个鼻子	a nose	yí gè bí zi	jat[1] go[3] bei[6] zi[2]
一个橙子	an orange	yí gè chéng zi	jat[1] go[3] caang[2] zi[2]
一个西瓜	a water melon	yí gè xī guā	jat[1] go[3] sai[1] gwaa[1]
一个苹果	an apple	yí gè píng guǒ	jat[1] go[3] ping[4] gwo[2]
一个梨	a pear	yí gè lí	jat[1] go[3] lei[2]
一个香蕉	a banana	yì gè xiāng jiāo	jat[1] go[3] hoeng[1] ziu[1]
一条		yì tiáo	jat[1] tiu[4]
一条裤子	a pair of trousers	yì tiáo kù zi	jat[1] tiu[4] fu[3] zi[2]
一条裙子	a skirt	yì tiáo qún zi	jat[1] tiu[4] kwan[4] zi[2]
一条鱼	a fish	yì tiáo yú	jat[1] tiu[4] jyu[4]
一件		yí jiàn	jat[1] gin[6]
一件毛衣	a jumper	yí jiàn máo yī	jat[1] gin[6] mou[4] ji[1]
一件汗衫	a T-shirt	yí jiàn hàn shān	jat[1] gin[6] hon[6] saam[1]

Vocabulary	English meaning	Putonghua pinyin	Cantonese jyutping
一双	a pair	yì shuāng	jat¹ soeng¹
一双鞋子	a pair of shoes	yì shuāng xié zi	jat¹ soeng¹ haai⁴ zi²
一双眼睛	a pair of eyes	yì shuāng yǎn jing	jat¹ soeng¹ ngaan⁵ zing¹
一双耳朵	a pair of ears	yì shuāng ěr duo	jat¹ soeng¹ ji⁵ do²
一双手	a pair of hands	yì shuāng shǒu	jat¹ soeng¹ sau²
一双脚	a pair of feet	yì shuāng jiǎo	jat¹ soeng¹ goek³
一只		yì zhī	jat¹ zek³
一只猫	a cat	yì zhī māo	jat¹ zek³ maau¹
一只狗	a dog	yì zhī gǒu	jat¹ zek³ gau²
一只鸟	a bird	yì zhī niǎo	jat¹ zek³ niu⁵
一头		yì tóu	jat¹ tau⁴
一头牛	a cow	yì tóu niú	jat¹ tau⁴ ngau⁴

齐来学中文丛书 基础课本
Let's Learn Chinese Series (Foundation Level)

编者 Written by:
英国中文学校联会 教育委员会教材编写小组
The Editorial of the Education Committee, UKFCS

美术 Illustrated by:
陈佩珊 Poi Chin
版式设计 Graphic Design by:
点睛龙创作室（澳大利亚）Dot Your I's Pty Limited (Australia)
排版、封面设计 Cover design by:
点睛龙创作室（澳大利亚）Dot Your I's Pty Limited (Australia)

出版发行 Published by:
英国中文学校联会 UK Federation of Chinese Schools
www.ukfcs.info
通讯地址 Correspondence address:
13 Langdale Close, Maidenhead, Berks SL6 1SY, England

印刷 Printed by:
Waterwell Media UK Ltd, 277B Abbeydale Road,
Wembley, Middlesex HA0 1TW, England

2008 年第一版 First published in Great Britain 2008

版权所有 不准翻印
Copyright © 2008 UKFCS
All rights reserved. No part of this publication may be reproduced in any form without permission from the publisher.

ISBN 978-1-906785-02-4

Cantonese	Jyutping					
CHAPTER 1	nei^5	nei^5 mun^4	hou^2	nei^3 hou^2	lou^5 si^1	zoi^3 gin^3
jat^1	ji^6	saam^1	sei^3	ng^5	luk^6	cat^1
baat^8	gau^2	sap^6				
CHAPTER 2	ngo^5	giu^3	ngo^5 giu^3	nei^5 giu^3	saam^6 mo^1	nei^5 giu^3
saam^6 mo^1	baak^6 sik^1	haak^1 sik^1				
CHAPTER 3	ngo^5 dik^1	gaa^1	jau^5	baa^1 baa^1	maa^1 maa^1	go^1 go^1
ze^2 ze^2	dai^6 dai^6	mui^6 mui^6	wo^4	go^3	jat^1 go^3	go^1 go^1
saam^1 go^3	ze^2 ze^2	sei^3 go^3	dai^6 dai^6	ng^5 go^3	mui^6 mui^6	
CHAPTER 4	seoi^3	gei^2 seoi^3	mut^6 jau^5	taa^1	taa^1	gei^2
nei^5 gei^2 seoi^3	ngo^5 luk^6 seoi^3	nei^5 jau^5 gei^2	go^3 go^1 go^1	jat^1 go^3	maa^1	nei^5 jau^5
mui^4 mui^2 maa^1	jau^5					
CHAPTER 5	ze^2	si^6	ze^2 si^6	ngo^5 dik^1	pang^4 jau^5	ngo^5 mun^4
hou^2 pang^4 yau^5	seoi^4	ze^5 si^6 seoi^4	ze^5 si^6 ngo^3	dik^1 dai^4 dai^2	seoi^4 dik^1	ze^5 si^6 seoi^4
dik^1 ze^4 ze^1	ze^5 si^6	Lei^5 Ping^4 dik^1	ze^4 ze^1			
CHAPTER 6	ngaan^4 sik^1	hung^4 sik^1	caang^2 sik^1	wong^4 sik^1	luk^6 sik^1	laam^4 sik^1
haak^1 sik^1	baak^6 sik^1	hei^2 fun^1				
CHAPTER 7	haai^4 zi^2	hon^6 saam^1	fu^3 zi^2	mou^4 ji^1	kwan^4 zi^2	jat^1 tiu^4
fu^3 zi^2	jat^1 gin^6	mou^4 ji^1	hon^6 saam^1	jat^1 soeng^1	haai^4 zi^2	
CHAPTER 8	maau^1	gau^2	ngau^4	joeng^4	niu^5	jyu^4
taa^1	jat^1 zek^3	maau^1	gau^2	niu^5	jat^1 tiu^4	jyu^4
jat^1 tau^4	ngau^4	joeng^4				
CHAPTER 9	ngaan^5 zing^1	ji^5 do^2	bei^6 zi^2	hau^2	sau^2	goek^3
ze^2 leoi^5	zoi^6	jat^1 go^3	hau^2	bei^6 zi^2	jat^1 soeng^1	ngaan^5 zing^1
ji^5 do^2	sau^2	goek^3	naa^3 leoi^5	nei^5 dik^1	ngaan^5 zing^1	zoi^6 naa^3 leoi^5
CHAPTER 10	hek^3	seoi^2 gwo^2	ping^4 gwo^2	sai^1 gwaa^1	lei^2	cou^2 mui^2

hoeng¹ ziu¹	caang²	jat¹ zek³	hoeng¹ ziu¹	jat¹ go³	caang²	sai¹ gwaa¹
ping⁴ gwo²	lei²	sam⁶ mo¹	sam⁶ mo¹	seoi² gwo²	hek³ sam⁶ mo¹	seoi² gwo²
nei⁵ hei² fun¹	hek³ sam⁶ mo¹	seoi² gwo²				
CHRISTMAS	sing³ daan³	zit³	sing³ daan³	lou⁵ jan⁴	sing³ daan³	syu⁶
daai⁶ gaa¹	faai³ lok⁶	lai⁵ mat⁶	paai³	coeng³ go¹		
NEW YEAR	san¹ nin⁴	tong⁴ gwo²	hung⁴ baau¹	zung¹ gwok³	san¹ nin⁴	nin⁴ gou¹
zung¹ gwok³						

Putonghua Pinyin

CHAPTER 1	nǐ	nǐ men	hǎo	nǐ hǎo	lǎo shī	zài jiàn
yī	èr	sān	sì	wǔ	liù	qī
bā	jiǔ	shí				
CHAPTER 2	wǒ	jiào	wǒ jiào	nǐ jiào	shén me	nǐ jiào
shén me	bái sè	hēi sè				
CHAPTER 3	wǒ de	jiā	yǒu	bà ba	mā ma	gē ge
jiě jie	dì di	mèi mei	hé	gè	yí gè	gē ge
sān gè	jiě jie	sì gè	dì di	wǔ gè	mèi mei	
CHAPTER 4	suì	jǐ suì	méi yǒu	tā	tā	jǐ
nǐ jǐ suì	wǒ liù suì	nǐ yǒu jǐ	gè gē ge	yí gè	ma	nǐ yǒu
mèi mei ma	yǒu					
CHAPTER 5	zhè	shì	zhè shì	wǒ de	péng yǒu	wǒ men
hǎo péng yǒu	shéi	zhè shì shéi	zhè shì wǒ	de dì di	shéi de	zhè shì shéi
de jiě jie	zhè shì	Lǐ Píng de	jiě jie			
CHAPTER 6	yán sè	hóng sè	chéng sè	huáng sè	lǜ sè	lán sè
hēi sè	bái sè	xǐ huān				
CHAPTER 7	xié zi	hàn shān	kù zi	máo yī	qún zi	yì tiáo